The Corgi and the Queen

Written by

Caroline L. Perry

Illustrated by

Lydia Corry

Henry Holt and Company
New York

E LIZABETH OF YORK wasn't a storybook princess.

Her younger sister, Margaret, loved playing dress-up in their mother's fancy gowns and twirling around her room in a diamond tiara.

But Elizabeth was happiest wearing normal clothes and playing fetch with the family's dogs, Dookie and Jane.

She spent afternoons at the stable grooming her Shetland pony, Peggy.

"You should have been a farm girl instead of a princess," Margaret teased.

When Elizabeth was only eleven years old, her life changed forever.
Her father was crowned King George VI.

The family moved into the grandest house in the nation.

Buckingham Palace was a cold, drafty place.

The floorboards creaked when Elizabeth, Margaret, and the dogs snuck off to explore the seven hundred and seventy-five rooms.

They peeked into echoey chambers with ornate ceilings, and gaped at portraits of royal ancestors adorning the walls.

They were scared to touch the priceless antique furnishings.

It was a truly magnificent residence. But it certainly wasn't homey.

People bowed and curtsied in King George's presence.
Everyone called him "Your Majesty."

He was just "Papa" to Elizabeth.
But Papa said that his little "Lilibet" would have to get used to all the fuss.
Someday, she would be queen.

The King and Queen traveled the world.
They went away for weeks, sometimes
months, at a time.

Elizabeth and Margaret
stayed behind.

A queen-in-waiting was expected to be perfect at all times.
But Dookie and Jane didn't have to worry about being "proper."

The feisty Pembroke Welsh corgis had no
regard for royal rules. They barked at the
princesses' stern governesses.

They chased palace servants around the great halls,
and wrestled when world leaders came to visit.

Elizabeth wished that she,
too, could go wild sometimes.

When Elizabeth was thirteen, World War II broke out in Europe.
For their safety, the princesses were sent away from London to Windsor Castle.
The King and Queen stayed at Buckingham Palace.
Even in their new home, Elizabeth and Margaret often woke to the loud shrill of
air-raid sirens.

They huddled together in the underground vaults of the castle,
behind hatboxes and cookie jars that hid the priceless Crown Jewels.
It was freezing cold, and the girls were lonely and scared.
The dogs never left their sides.

War was still raging when Elizabeth turned eighteen.

Papa told her she could choose any gift her heart desired.

"You must ask for a car!" Margaret urged.

"Fine jewelry, fit for a princess," Mama suggested.

"A new royal title," palace advisers proposed.

Elizabeth asked for only one thing.
"I want a puppy of my own!" she declared.

The princess got her wish: a corgi pup she named Susan.

Elizabeth's heart swelled when she cuddled the tiny dog.
It wasn't easy for a future queen to make friends.
At last, she had her very own constant companion.

Susan was small but rambunctious.

She loved to show off her herding skills.

There weren't any sheep at the castle, so she rounded up squirrels.

When enemy planes flew overhead she growled, and guarded the princess like a precious lamb.

Elizabeth was captivated by the little corgi.
She hand-fed her from a silver platter and
walked her twice each day.

She told Susan stories and stroked
the puppy's soft belly.

The princess had learned to
bury her emotions.
But somehow, Susan knew
exactly how she was feeling.

The corgi nuzzled close when Elizabeth argued with her sister.

Susan dropped toys at the princess's feet to cheer her up during long, boring lessons on constitutional history.

She comforted her companion when the sounds of battle kept them awake at night.

Having Susan at her side gave Elizabeth courage.

She pleaded with Papa to let her join the war effort.

"It isn't fitting for a future queen!" royal advisers wailed.

"I'm not an ordinary princess," Elizabeth insisted. "And I have no intention of being an ordinary queen."

She knew that she had to help her country.

Eventually, the King relented, and Elizabeth joined a women's regiment.

She learned how to be a mechanic, and she drove military trucks and ambulances.

She became an expert at changing tires and fixing engines.

Elizabeth returned to Windsor Castle each night exhausted and covered in grease.

Her dressers winced when they saw her oil-smudged face and filthy overalls.

But Susan always leapt into Elizabeth's arms.
The loyal corgi didn't care about her appearance.
The princess knew that her beloved pet was proud of her.

At last, the war was over.

Back at Buckingham Palace, the dogs lived like royalty.
They moved into their own special "corgi room."
At bedtime, they curled up in cozy wicker baskets,
raised off the ground to avoid chilly drafts.

Their sheets were changed every day.

They ate gourmet food, prepared by palace chefs.

Elizabeth took care of all the dogs.

She even made each pet a treat-filled stocking at Christmas.

But Susan was the apple of her eye.

Not everyone loved Susan as much as the princess did.

"OWWWWW!" the royal clock winder yelped when the dog nipped him on the bottom, ripping a hole in his pants.

"OUT!" the King yelled when Susan snuck into the State Dining Room and stole filet mignon from his plate.

"AAAHHHHHH!" Margaret screamed when she
stepped on a live mouse that Susan had hidden inside her jeweled slipper.

The corgi was often in the doghouse.
But Elizabeth always took her side.

Twenty-year-old Elizabeth had fallen in love.

Philip Mountbatten was handsome and kind, and the future queen was smitten.

But before she accepted Philip's proposal, she had to be sure of one thing.

Would Susan like him?

The corgi snarled at people she didn't
care for, but Philip petted her gently.
She fell asleep at his feet.
Susan approved.

Elizabeth's wedding was the most lavish event of the decade.

Extravagant gifts arrived from all corners of the globe.

They filled an entire room at the palace!

Invitations were sent to two thousand viscounts, VIPs, duchesses, and dames.

But the princess's closest companion wasn't on the guest list.

Elizabeth's ladies-in-waiting hatched a plan
to make Susan a secret part of the celebrations.

After the ceremony on November 20, 1947, the newlyweds rode across London in an elegant glass coach.

Hundreds of thousands of well-wishers lined the streets.

Their chants were deafening!

Adults and children waited for hours, hoping to catch a glimpse of the radiant royal bride.

Not one of them realized that Susan was a stowaway in the gilded carriage, hidden beneath a handwoven rug on the floor.

Palace staff had smuggled the dog on board with a stash of special treats and a hot-water bottle to keep her warm.

While waving at the jubilant crowds, Elizabeth could feel Susan playing at her feet. On the biggest day of her life, she had her best friend by her side.

The following year Elizabeth
gave birth to a son, Charles.

Susan also became a mom.
She had two puppies, named Sugar
and Honey.
The corgis traveled everywhere with
the princess and her young family.
Susan protected all of the babies in
the royal residence.

When Elizabeth was only twenty-five, her
father passed away.

In a grand ceremony, she was crowned
Queen Elizabeth II.

Millions watched the royal coronation, and the
world cheered for the beautiful young monarch.

Elizabeth smiled for the cameras.

A queen couldn't cry in public.

But she sobbed for her papa when she was
alone with Susan.

Elizabeth soon learned how to be a great ruler.

She welcomed people from all nations and faiths into her home.

She worked hard to promote kindness and bridge divides.

Susan was always by her side.

But one cold January day, the barking stopped.

The Queen buried Susan on the grounds of the Sandringham Estate,

where her playful dog had loved to run and chase pigeons.

Elizabeth chose the inscription for Susan's headstone:

"For almost 15 years, the faithful companion of the Queen."

No British monarch ruled longer than Queen Elizabeth II.

Over the course of her long life and her remarkable seventy-year reign, the Queen had at least thirty corgi companions.

"My corgis are family," she has said.

Fourteen generations of her cherished dogs were descended from Susan.

Elizabeth never forgot the corgi who helped a young
princess learn how to become a beloved queen.
Elizabeth's and Susan's legacies live on.

FAMILY TREE OF QUEEN ELIZABETH II

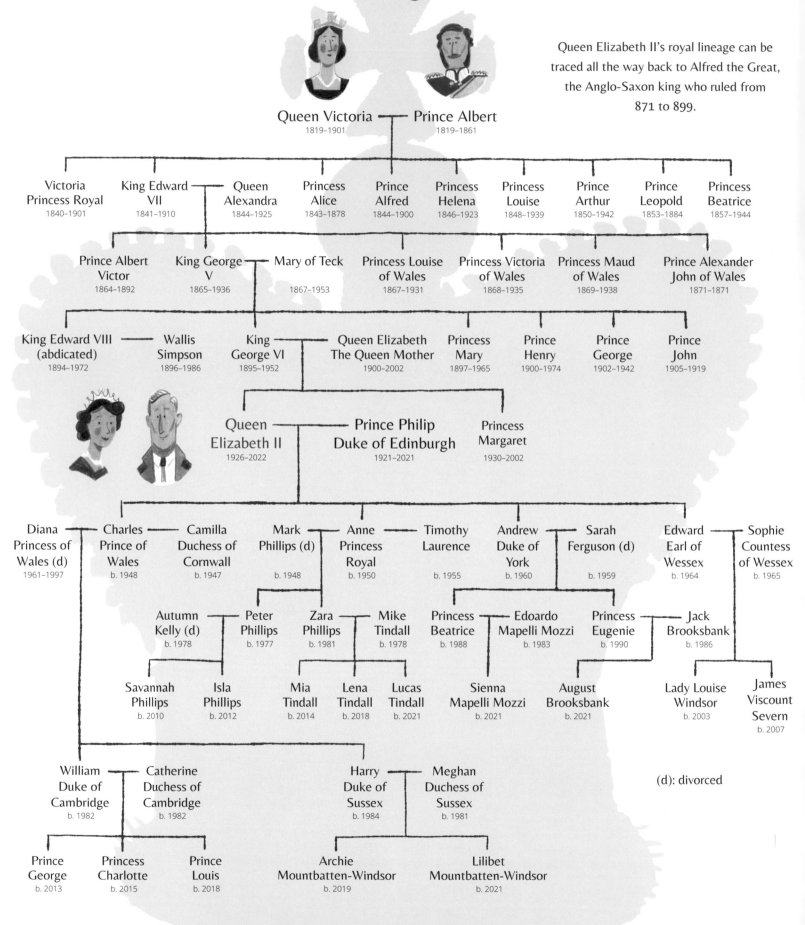

Queen Elizabeth II's royal lineage can be traced all the way back to Alfred the Great, the Anglo-Saxon king who ruled from 871 to 899.

Queen Victoria 1819–1901 — Prince Albert 1819–1861

Victoria Princess Royal 1840–1901 | King Edward VII 1841–1910 — Queen Alexandra 1844–1925 | Princess Alice 1843–1878 | Prince Alfred 1844–1900 | Princess Helena 1846–1923 | Princess Louise 1848–1939 | Prince Arthur 1850–1942 | Prince Leopold 1853–1884 | Princess Beatrice 1857–1944

Prince Albert Victor 1864–1892 | King George V 1865–1936 — Mary of Teck 1867–1953 | Princess Louise of Wales 1867–1931 | Princess Victoria of Wales 1868–1935 | Princess Maud of Wales 1869–1938 | Prince Alexander John of Wales 1871–1871

King Edward VIII (abdicated) 1894–1972 — Wallis Simpson 1896–1986 | King George VI 1895–1952 — Queen Elizabeth The Queen Mother 1900–2002 | Princess Mary 1897–1965 | Prince Henry 1900–1974 | Prince George 1902–1942 | Prince John 1905–1919

Queen Elizabeth II 1926–2022 — Prince Philip Duke of Edinburgh 1921–2021 | Princess Margaret 1930–2002

Diana Princess of Wales (d) 1961–1997 — Charles Prince of Wales b. 1948 — Camilla Duchess of Cornwall b. 1947 | Mark Phillips (d) b. 1948 — Anne Princess Royal b. 1950 — Timothy Laurence b. 1955 | Andrew Duke of York b. 1960 — Sarah Ferguson (d) b. 1959 | Edward Earl of Wessex b. 1964 — Sophie Countess of Wessex b. 1965

Autumn Kelly (d) b. 1978 — Peter Phillips b. 1977 | Zara Phillips b. 1981 — Mike Tindall b. 1978 | Princess Beatrice b. 1988 — Edoardo Mapelli Mozzi b. 1983 | Princess Eugenie b. 1990 — Jack Brooksbank b. 1986

Savannah Phillips b. 2010 | Isla Phillips b. 2012 | Mia Tindall b. 2014 | Lena Tindall b. 2018 | Lucas Tindall b. 2021 | Sienna Mapelli Mozzi b. 2021 | August Brooksbank b. 2021 | Lady Louise Windsor b. 2003 | James Viscount Severn b. 2007

(d): divorced

William Duke of Cambridge b. 1982 — Catherine Duchess of Cambridge b. 1982 | Harry Duke of Sussex b. 1984 — Meghan Duchess of Sussex b. 1981

Prince George b. 2013 | Princess Charlotte b. 2015 | Prince Louis b. 2018 | Archie Mountbatten-Windsor b. 2019 | Lilibet Mountbatten-Windsor b. 2021

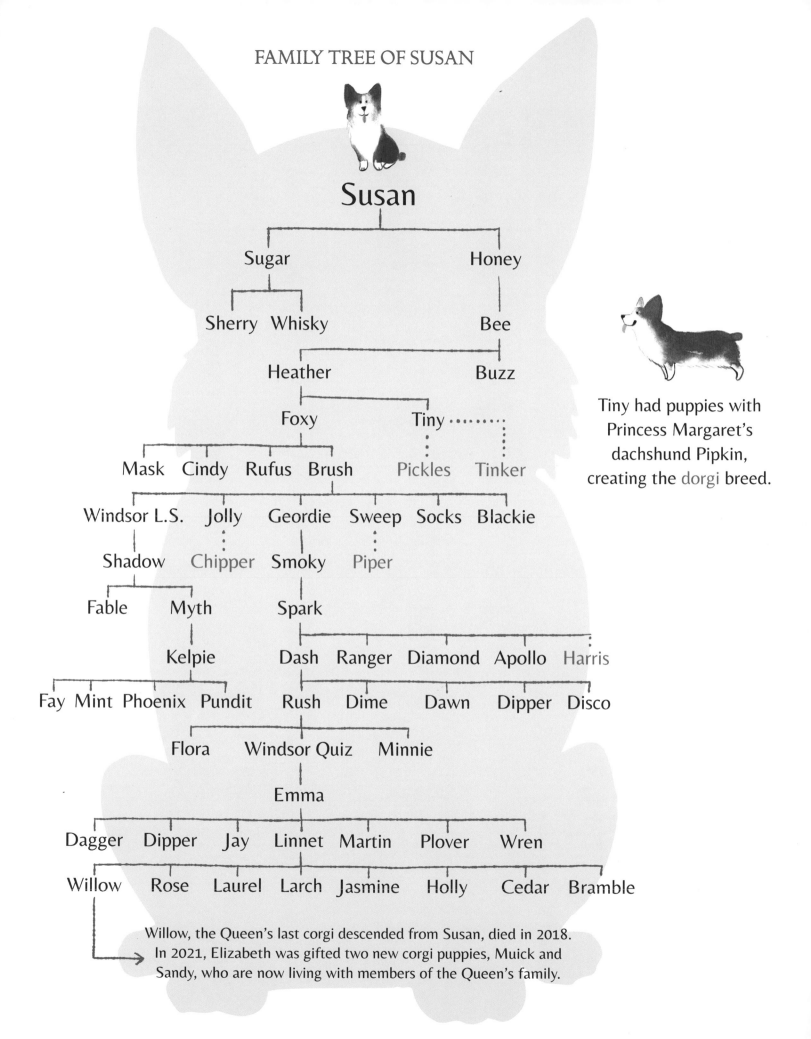

FAMILY TREE OF SUSAN

Susan
- Sugar
  - Sherry
  - Whisky
- Honey
  - Bee

- Heather
  - Foxy
    - Mask
    - Cindy
    - Rufus
    - Brush
  - Tiny
    - Pickles
    - Tinker
- Buzz

- Windsor L.S.
  - Shadow
    - Fable
    - Myth
      - Kelpie
        - Fay
        - Mint
        - Phoenix
        - Pundit
- Jolly
  - Chipper
- Geordie
  - Smoky
    - Spark
      - Dash
        - Rush
      - Ranger
      - Diamond
      - Apollo
      - Harris
- Sweep
  - Piper
- Socks
- Blackie

- Dime
- Dawn
- Dipper
- Disco

- Flora
- Windsor Quiz
- Minnie

- Emma
  - Dagger
  - Dipper
  - Jay
  - Linnet
  - Martin
  - Plover
  - Wren

- Willow
- Rose
- Laurel
- Larch
- Jasmine
- Holly
- Cedar
- Bramble

Tiny had puppies with Princess Margaret's dachshund Pipkin, creating the dorgi breed.

Willow, the Queen's last corgi descended from Susan, died in 2018. In 2021, Elizabeth was gifted two new corgi puppies, Muick and Sandy, who are now living with members of the Queen's family.

For Oscar, Leo, and Eloise, the jewels in my crown,
and for my majestic mum, Angela —C. L. P.

For my father Adrian, with all my love —L. C.

Henry Holt and Company, *Publishers since 1866*
Henry Holt® is a registered trademark of Macmillan Publishing Group, LLC
120 Broadway, New York, NY 10271 • mackids.com

Our books may be purchased in bulk for promotional, educational, or business use.
Please contact your local bookseller or the Macmillan Corporate and Premium Sales Department at
(800) 221-7945 ext. 5442 or by email at MacmillanSpecialMarkets@macmillan.com.

Library of Congress Control Number: 2022910406

First Edition, 2022
Book design by Aram Kim and Melisa Vuong
The illustrations for this book were created with watercolor, gouache, and pencil on paper.
Printed in United States of America by Phoenix Color, Hagerstown, Maryland

ISBN 978-1-250-83238-2
3 5 7 9 10 8 6 4